Under Ducor Skies

Under Ducor Skies

Patrice D. Juah

Poems

VILLAGE TALES PUBLISHING | USA

A catalog record for this book is available from the Library of Congress:
LCCN: 2018953477
ISBN: 9781945408212
eISBN: 9781945408229

Published By:
Village Tales Publishing
Lawrenceville, GA

Layout and Cover Design by: OASS
Author's photo by Nii Lightville Djarbeng

www.villagetalespublishing.com
www.oass.villagetalespublishing.com

Printed in the United States of America

Dedication

To my mother, Martha Juah,
for igniting the flame, and my big sister
and backup mom, Oretha Juah (O.J),
for carrying the torch.

"Wander, wild and free, far and wide in search of your home. That place where your soul finds peace. That place where you're appreciated, celebrated and loved."
~ Patrice Juah

Contents

LIB, The Place To Be   11
Africa's Cry   13
Angelic Stranger   15
I Wish I Were An Angel   16
I'm Doing Me   17
Fistula, I Have Conquered You!   19
A Lion With A Heart Of Gold   21
A Treasure In Queechee   23
My Black Bra And I   25
Where The Rivers Dance   27
Why I Travel   29
The Hanover Drought   31
The Ebola Ride   34
Celebrate Women, Celebrate!   37
They Sailed Away   39
The Flower Story   41
My Journey   43
Step Out Girl   44
A Thousand Lives   45
Woman On A Mission   46
My Body, My Pride   48
Suddenly   50
Nothing Can Tell How I Feel   51
Painful Christmas   52
Beyond Doubts   53
They Called Me Mama Africa   54
Her Mind Grew Wings   55
Discuss Your Life   56
Education, I Cherish You   57
You Remain 16 To Me   58
My Child I Never Got to Meet   60
Sorry I Left You Behind   62
When Love Is Not Enough   64
Waiting   66
We Are Here   67
That Thing Called Fear   68
I Cannot Help But Shine   69

Make Your Behind-the-Scenes Beautiful   70
To Love An ECOWAS Passport Holder   71
Prayer Of Humility 72
Even If   73
My Own Identity   74
The Glorious Stage   76
Wish Of A Dreamer   77
On A Rainy Day   78
Friends Of The World   79
Tell Your Story   80
These Daughters Of Ours   82
My Sisters In Goals, Strength And Prayers 83
The Lonestar Rant   84
When I Turned 30   87
On Planes   88
Riding Through Africa   89
Voice In A Hole   90
Love Like This   92
The Day I Found You   93
Liberia   94
Life   96
A True Friend   97
Under Ducor Skies   98
Married To Me   99
I'm Liberian 100
Let's Rebuild Liberia Together   102
The African Dream 105
Take Me To Kpatawee   106
Not An Ordinary Woman   107
About the Author   110

Acknowledgment

Many thanks to God Almighty, without whom none of this would have been possible. I thank Him for wisdom and guidance, and for endowing me with the beautiful gift of writing. I thank Him wholeheartedly for the platform to birth and share it with the world. To Him alone be all the glory.

I also thank my beloved mother, Ma Martha, an educator and woman of faith, for planting the seeds of education, hard work and discipline in me from a young age.

My gratitude goes out to my darling big sister and backup mom, Oretha, for nurturing my talents, believing in me, and being an anchor of strength and support over the years. I'm grateful to my entire family for their prayers, encouragement, and support.

I'd like to thank the Liberia Association of Writers (LAW), for amplifying my confidence in my writing, by giving me my first real platform as a teenage writer, through the National High School Poetry Competition they organized, which I won, at the age of 16.

A big thank you to my high school English teacher at the time, Mr. Edwin Flahn Harris, for encouraging me to take my gift of writing from my high school morning devotion, to a bigger stage—LAW's poetry competition.

My principal at St. Teresa Convent Catholic High School, Ms. Lena Pearl Carey, I say a big thank you to you for listening to, and believing in my poems, and creating several platforms to share them with my schoolmates.

To audiences that have listened to me read, recite, or perform my poetry, and later asked if I had a book; or where they could get my book; I say thank you for motivating me to bring this book to life.

Ms. Ophelia S. Lewis and the Village Tales Publishing family; thank you isn't enough to express how grateful I am for your support and guidance throughout this process. Thank you for believing in my work and bringing it to life.

To my young mentees, who, instead of inspiring them, continue to inspire me, with their brilliance, resilience, and determination, I say thank you. A massive thank you to everyone that has prayed for me, supported me and given me an opportunity or platform to shine and share my work. To God be the glory.

LIB, The Place To Be

I

They call it LIB[1],
I call it the place to be.
Nowhere else I'd rather be,
But right here in LIB.
I know it's bumpy;
Sometimes, even, rocky.
The hustle takes the pressure high
And we often sigh,
But if that's the definition of pain,
I can endure it, just to be in LIB.

II

A land of beauty and resilience;
Budding cultures and vibrant spirits.
Who can ever ignore her hospitable embrace?
Oil palm and mangrove swamps;
Cool December Harmattan Wind,
Dust-filled nostrils and 'Yanlaypaypay[2]'—laden skin,
But all the same, the beach is within my reach.
Mangoes and sugarcane,
Groundpea, butterpear
And cassava leaves.
They're always in haste,
To savor the taste of LIB.

---

1   LIB - nickname for Liberia.
2   Yanlaypaypay - fun Liberian nickname for dryness of
the skin, caused by the harmattan wind.

III

Hipco[3], Gbehma[4], Pen-pen[5]—yes, that's LIB!
Years of war and intruder Ebola
Could not dim the light of Africa's Lonestar.
Rushing rivers and sunny skies;
Too different to ignore, too unique to copy.
Streets littered with humor
And wisdom from young and old,
Sasa and drums, resounding stories untold.
I travel far and wide,
But every new path takes me back to LIB.
Normal days are back,
So join me in LIB, the place to be.

---

3   HipCo - genre of Liberian music; a mix of Hip-hop and Liberian colloquial.
4   Gbehma - traditional music genre in Liberia.
5   Pen-Pen - nickname for commercial motorbikes in Liberia

Africa's Cry

I

Down, down, in the sandy Sahara,
Up the Mount Kilimanjaro to Lake Victoria,
From north to south
And east to west ;
From morning till night,
From dusk to dawn,
I hear Africa's Cry.

Why should she be tormented?
Why should she be humiliated,
And Strangulated by war and poverty?

II

Africa's crying,
Drenched with blood and covered with wounds;
She's faint and weary.
Starvation, diseases, and instability
Have become the inhabitants of her land,
Her resources, now enemies that destroy her.
Political unrests and insecurity
Are the companions that guide her steps.

III

Oh Africa! Mama Africa,
The roaring continent is crying;
Cries of sorrow, pain and anguish.
I can hear the echoes from the mountains and valleys.
She says she wants peace—not war,
Security—not insecurity.
She says she's tired of being oppressed;
She says she's still in slavery,
And wants to be free forever.

IV

Africa's crying,
Her tears keep flowing,
Her wounds are bleeding.
She's crying,
Crying for peace, justice,
Freedom and love.

Angelic Stranger

Swept away by a stranger,
Tall, dark and handsome.
He came fully armed,
With weapons strong enough
To knock down walls.

Gaze so intense,
Hearts could melt from a single stare.
Arms so protective,
One could drown in his embrace.
Kiss so warm,
Gives heat on a rainy day.

He walked boldly
To a gated and chained heart;
Determined to possess its key.
Immersed in his warmth and passion,
She stood in awe and doubt.

Is it worth the risk?
Her head or heart must decide.
Should he take the key?
Should she give him the key?
A battle of fear
And feelings unexplained.

Let the answers wander,
Until the wind blows them,
Cause at that very moment,
They only cared to savor the spark
That shone between them,

As they stood at crossroads,
At her heart's gate.

I Wish I Were An Angel

If I were an angel,
I'd fly with my wings,
And sleep with you in your bed.

If I could just become an angel,
You and I would see how the sun sets,
And how the moon lights up the sky.

If I were an angel,
I'd follow you every step of the way,
And cover you with my wings of love.

If I were an angel,
I'd kiss your lips,
And leave honey on them.

If I were an angel,
I'd fly with you up in the sky,
And we would never stop looking
Into each other's eyes.

If I were an angel,
You and I would build a mansion up in the clouds,
And love would be our radiant light.

I wish I were an angel for you.

I'm Doing Me

I saw these shoes,
They looked so fly,
I took a sigh and decided to buy.
They're pricey—yes!
Don't ask me why,
Cause I'm doing me.

My weave's so long,
Like an entire song,
It gives my shoes a wink,
And together they blink.
They've all gotten the message,
And know without a doubt,
I'm doing me.

My arm's tired, from carrying this classy tote,
And whispers "Can't she quit?"
My silky long weave gives it a gentle caress,
And it cares less;
Because it knows that
I'm doing me.

My glamorous hat adorns my head,
Who said I can't?
Please take that back,
I'm doing me.

My sunglasses know the fierceness of my eyes,
Just a stare and you're under my spell.
They keep the secret without a doubt,
By now, they're more than aware that,
I'm doing Me.

I enter a room,
My cherry lips bloom,

The air freezes;
Everyone stands still.
My fragrance takes over,
They inhale,
All that makes me an enchanting woman,
And instantly know that,
I'm doing me.

Make up done, nails done—sparkling!
All part of the "Me Team,"
They stay on track,
No secrets spilled,
Cause I'm in charge,
I'm doing me!

Fistula, I Have Conquered You!
(In honor of the survivors of Obstetric Fistula)

It was a lonely road,
I watched as you invaded my body.
An unwelcomed guest, determined to stay.
You didn't give me the chance
To grow up into the woman
I dreamt of becoming.

You dug a hole
That drained away my confidence,
Self-worth and pride.
You turned life's precious moments
That should have brought joy,
Into moments of pain, shame and anguish.

You seized my freedom,
And imprisoned me with humiliation.
Nobody saw my gentle and caring heart,
Nobody saw my potential.
I was only remembered
For the filth and stench I carried around.

You turned "happily ever after"
Into "oh no, I should have never!"
You made me look
Into the eyes of my newborn child
With blame and regrets, instead of love.

You turned my dreams into nightmares.
This journey continued,
Until I came to a place of enlightenment;
A place of awareness,
A place of hope and education;
With possibilities to start anew.

Like loose chains,
My fears began to break.
Like sand on the sea shore,
My ignorance was erased.
And then I realized,
That you are only as strong
As I make you seem.

Fistula, I Have Conquered You!
I've broken every barrier you've made,
And have set my mind and body free!
I now stand healthy and strong!

I'm now a woman
Society no longer ridicules,
But embraces.
I no longer bow my head in shame.

Through awareness,
I'm fully armed and equipped!
I breathe a new air.
Today, I can boldly look you in the eye and say:
"Fistula, I have conquered you!"

A Lion With A Heart Of Gold

In honor of President Barack Obama, July 28, 2014—YALI
Presidential Summit, Washington, D.C.

We stood in awe as he entered the room,
To grace our hearts with his powerful presence.
Overwhelmed with joy we looked on;
Beaming with smiles and excitement,
As thoughts of what he'd say,
And how he'd be, filled our minds.

I wondered if he'd be the same cool guy
I watched on television
From my little corner of Africa,
For hours unending, in 2008,
In anticipation of history's dawn.

For whom I had bought
Gallons of gasoline
To keep my generator beating,
Through Monrovia's dark skies;
To watch this Lion finally take his throne,
A celebration of that long awaited dream.

It felt like I knew him, like we were family.
One word uttered and
Everything began to bloom.
He stood there,
The very definition of charisma.

That powerful presence,
That glowing, yet knowing smile;
Oh, I could not believe my eyes!
That confident walk,
Those regal steps!

It was truly happening
And I was there,
In the midst of it all.
Savoring, dreaming,
And beaming with hope.

His wit makes the weight of the struggles light.
A strong Lion whose heart is pure Gold.
His words,
Resounding with wisdom of stories untold.
Is he truly one of us?
Yes, he is;
Or so he makes us feel,
With that all too familiar grin.

A lion whose heart
Is adorned with the finest Gold,
His humor, too surreal to be real;
But then he's real, so that's just him,
A Lion with a heart of Gold.

He feels our pain and knows our stories,
Far beyond what we know.
With him by our side,
We feel empowered in our fight
To end poverty, corruption,
And all forms of injustice.

And here we are today,
Drowning in these blessings,
Because of the most beautiful gift
He's given to Africa; the gift that YALI is.
We're Young African Leaders;
Equipped with the task
Of steering his vision for Africa,
For years to come.

A Treasure In Queechee

I travelled far and wide,
Valleys low and mountains high,
Through thick jungles and soaring planes,
I kept on searching for what was missing.

The days were dark and the nights were bright,
Confusion, delusion—lost!
My search continued across oceans,
As I moved by life's motions.

In this misery awaited a story,
Of a lost treasure I'd someday find;
Answers to questions long buried,
In a faraway land.

One sunny day,
The waters swept those Liberian shores
And took me to Quechee, Vermont,
A place I'd never dreamed of.

I landed eyes closed,
Without a hint of what to expect;
Then soon opened my eyes
To what was paradise, true fairytale beauty!

And just when I wasn't looking,
I stumbled upon something priceless;
A treasure in Quechee, Vermont,
A glimpse of its glitter, sent answers flooding in.

That dull picture of the future became oh so clear,
As I sat in the valley, savoring
The picturesque Ottauquechee River;
Everything suddenly made sense.

I found a treasure in Quechee, Vermont,
One with which I'd longed to commune,
One that would define life's true meaning;
I found a treasure in Quechee, Vermont,
And that treasure is me.

My Black Bra And I

People will never understand what we have,
But my black bra and I have a love affair.
She holds me tight
When his hands are nowhere in sight,
With defiance, she gives me confidence
Holding the twins firm.

When his five kids, sent them falling
From "Perky land" to "Sagging land,"
She keeps them standing tall
And reassures me saying,
"You still got it girl,
Keep your head up."

Yes, we do talk,
And the special bond we share
Cannot be concealed.
My black bra and I
Surely have something deep going on.

Permanently dressed in black,
She mourns daily for all the hurt he caused,
And clings to me gently,
Caressing away the pain.

She's my girl,
And our intimacy is sheer bliss;
She knows and sees everything,
Secrets and all.

She hides all my scars,
And is first to smell every fragrance.
Her clip on my back;
A reminder that she's got me.

Her protective grip
Feels like his hands,
Except this time,
It's gentle and
I'm no longer that vulnerable girl;
So I relish in her every embrace.

We cannot kiss,
Or look into each other's eyes;
But what we share is oh so dear.
I feel safe and not betrayed,
Loved and not hurt.
I feel liberated every time she touches
And clings onto me.

Oh, did I mention
She saves me from going under the knife?
Yes, we know how to package the girls;
And that's our well-kept secret!

My black bra and I,
Have an unbreakable love affair
To last through the ages.

Where The Rivers Dance

Birds chirp away,
Children sing happily through their day,
As they sit by the fire hearth
Listening to tales of where the rivers dance.

Some say it is a woman,
Whose breasts gush out pure honey.
Some say it is a female hunter,
Triumphantly taking home
The catch of the day to feed her family.

Some say its rushing waters,
Echo the sounds of sasa and drums;
A whisper of trees in Kulangyea,
Waving their branches over Belefanai.

Some say it is a love affair
Of two sparkling streams,
Gliding in passion towards one powerful melody,
Before bursting into the sea;
Their offsprings weave beautiful pearls
Spun upon the earth's shores,
Adorning the necks of princesses and queens.

It's not just any river,
It's an African river;
Like Meng River,
Flowing beneath Yeakporwa in Zota,
Like Djor river,
Gliding peacefully through Gbarnga town.

There are songs of magic
Where the rivers dance;
Love stories are sealed,
Wounds are mended,

Battles are won,
And bonds are forged.

Where the rivers dance—
An African river,
A Liberian river;
Are stories of how
A nation triumphed over despair
Into an era of promise.

Why I Travel

Too often,
I'm asked why I travel so much.
At first it's irritating,
Later amusing,
And leaves me feeling sorry for those asking.
Sorry that they're probably
Sitting in some corner somewhere,
Letting life pass them by,
Or wishing and planning
For that 'one day' that may never come.

But it's a simple fact,
And not as complicated
As they make it seem.
I travel for work,
And sometimes for play;
To explore and discover.
I travel to fall in love,
Or sometimes,
To just heal my broken heart
With new and beautiful sceneries.

Sometimes to breathe and start afresh;
To reboot, refresh, learn, and unlearn.
I travel to re-connect with the universe;
To soothe away despair and reawaken my dreams.
I travel because there's a beautiful world
Outside the boundaries of my comfort zone,
Whose arms await me.
I travel to meet people—
New people, cool people.

People who aren't afraid to wander,
They know wandering only
Brings you closer to

That sacred place of purpose.
I travel to spread my wings
And soar across the plains of my limitations.
It is in soaring that
I get to rise above the depth of impossibilities
To new heights of hope.

I travel to find a lost treasure
Which I possessed all along,
But didn't know I had.
Every new flight,
Blue sky and green plain,
Leads me forward and closer
To finding that which I travelled miles to find—
Myself.

The Hanover Drought

(Inspired by my Mandela Washington Fellowship experience at Dartmouth College in Hanover, New Hampshire)

I

Brace yourselves oh people of Hanover,
For something unusual awaits this town.
A time of empty streets and slow paced cars,
Of dried flowers and sunburned leaves
No more eager and smiling faces to greet,
That time is near and,
You'll meet it with sorrow and cries.

"How can such disaster hit an affluent town?"
I hear you ask.
It's the Hanover Drought,
And it's like nothing you've ever seen.
When the foreign faces
On the Dartmouth Coach will be gone,
And the dining halls will
Bear no trace of their footsteps,
When CVS will be just another place for essentials,
And not a "fancy shopping mall."
When the once lively Lodge,
Will go dead with silence.

II

Watch out for the Hanover Drought,
When the streets will lose their vibrant colors
And eclectic tastes.
A time of "human recession,"
When the Connection Circles
And site visits will be no more,
When all the elements of Design Thinking,
Entrepreneurship and Leadership,
Will be shipped away to the African shores.

Are you ready for the Hanover Drought?
When the ideas once tweaked for weeks,
Will finally come to life on the African soil.
The Hanover Drought,
When all the YALI Fellows will be gone
To bless the continent of Africa because of you,
Dartmouth—the ever powerful Green.
The Hanover Drought,
An uncontrollable period of change,
When your lives will take a spin,
Before your very eyes.

III

Oh wait a minute,
You won't experience this alone,
We too will have our fair share
Of longing and grief,
As we reflect on the transformative journeys,
From Boston to Hanover;
From Vermont to Burlington;
"Killing babies[6]" and playing beer games,
Our professors' humor and wit,
Our awesome hosts;
The friendly faces that made this place home.
Though departing,
We'll always remain grateful to you
For enriching our lives,
In ways too deep to explain.

But the drought will suddenly disappear,
When the seeds you've planted
Begin to sprout forth across our Africa.
With pride you'll come to life again,
Knowing that everything you touch
Turns to gold. Then Hanover
Will experience her glory days once more,
All because of you, dear Dartmouth.

---

6   Killing babies: a term coined by Prof. Gregg Fairbrothers of Dartmouth College, to refer to the elimination of unprofitable ideas.

IV

The legacy of Thayer,
Tuck and Rockefeller,
Will live on in each of us for years to come,
Until our paths cross at the Big Green,
Where the Hanover Drought will be long forgotten;
Then together we shall all say,
UBUNTU, "I am because we are."

The Ebola Ride

On the Ebola ride,
Paranoia is the driver.
It takes you on a high
And leaves your senses
Hanging in the wild.

Fear is its deputy,
And panic, the conductor.
You never know
Which way the bus will go,
But you are told,
That as long as you stay put.

Wash your hands
And limit human contact;
You're safe, at least for a while.
You do your best
To secure your seat,
Making sure your loved ones
Are safely on board.

But as death news come in,
You're reminded,
This isn't a normal ride.
You get a sudden kick,
A silent voice asking,
Why you're still here;
Perhaps on a mission,
Or for a purpose?

Then suddenly gratitude takes over,
As you give thanks
For still being alive.
And this is all happening
On the Ebola ride.

Still on the road, pickups rush by
with men dressed like aliens,
Either carrying or going
To pick up fallen victims.
Somewhere in a Containment Unit,
A baby cries in horror,
As his mother takes her last breath.

You peek through the window,
Crowded streets create the illusion
Of a normal life, but as alive
As everything appears from the outside,
Fear is killing us slowly on the inside.

Sometimes we wonder
Who'll get off next,
But that's the Ebola ride:
No traffic lights, no horns,
No road signs,
Just us against an unseen enemy.

The night brings relative calm,
But we rarely sleep,
As the nightmare of
What's to come the day ahead
Haunts our dreams.

And on the other side,
The ocean wind sets the flames
In the Crematorium ablaze,
As our hearts leap
For the souls of the ones dearly loved—

No last goodbyes,
Only memories, anguish,
Pain and grief.
We're stuck on this bumpy ride,

With tiny doses of hope.
And though help arrives,
We're still in doubt,
As they too are clueless
About when the ride will end.

So world, we're here,
On this hand-washing,
Temperature-taking,
Emotion-wrecking,
Friends-avoiding,
Hugs and handshake-prohibiting,
Nonstop Ebola ride.

Celebrate Women, Celebrate!

For so long we were torn apart,
Our voices were buried in the cold dark earth,
Our songs were cries and our rain, tears;
We were silenced and banned
From speaking our truths.

Hate towards each other burdened us,
As fear crippled us.
We were blinded by lies
That tore our efforts into shreds.
We would form "Pity Parties,"
Wallow in sorrow and rejoice
Over each other's downfall.

Our hope was lost and our courage killed.
In all this misery,
Something happened on that fateful day,
The wind of change swept across our hearts,
And we could suddenly see
What strength sisterhood brings.

The chains were set loose
And left our hands free,
Free to unite and
Embrace one another.
Consumed by love we cried,
But tears of joy this time.

We began a new journey together,
And have stood strong
In spite of our differences.
We've cherished our uniqueness,
And dispelled the "myth" that we are weak.

Celebrate women, celebrate!
Celebrate how far we've come,
And how much further we must go.
Celebrate the resurrection
Of our voices to speak for the voiceless.

Celebrate ruling nations and touching lives.
Celebrate being mothers, daughters, sisters, wives,
Presidents, bosses and role models—
All in one dress.
Celebrate being heroines
In the fight to end injustice
And violence against women.

Give a smile in place of a frown,
Dance to the rhythm
Of the peace you helped to build.
Pat yourselves on the back
For a race perfectly run.
"W" marks the beginning of 'World',
Women make the world.
Celebrate women, celebrate!

They Sailed Away
(The Americo-Liberian story)

The wind blew,
Fresh air of freedom across their faces
As the plantation trees
Waved their final goodbyes.
From the rays of sunlight,
They walked triumphantly aboard
Elizabeth, The Mayflower—
The gateway to their old, yet new home.

A journey once made
In tears and chains by the ancestors,
Was now a journey of freedom.
They took one last glimpse
At the place they had come to call home,
A place whose memories
Would be forever etched in their minds;
From the hands of their oppressors,
They sailed away.

To the Grain Coast,
Where their troubles would be no more,
They sailed away;
To the land of their forefathers,
They sailed away.

With opened arms,
Those on the land embraced them.
In spite of their differences,
They shared the same blood.
Although they'd lost their names,
Their faces unmasked their identity.

In search of liberty,
They sailed away.

To mangrove swamps
And waving palm trees, they sailed away.
Once lost, they finally reclaimed their place;
Far away on Africa's western shores,
A place whose history they would shape.
Today, the streets carry their names,
And the anthem and drums
Echo hope through pain.

Through unity,
They built a nation—Liberia
Nearly torn apart,
They all sailed away
From fourteen years of devastation,
To a future of lasting peace.

The Flower Story

When you see a beautiful flower,
Stop and reflect,
Before basking in its beauty
And plucking it away.

Think about the many days
It went un-watered,
Was trampled upon and
Baked by the blazing sun.

Think about the thorns
That attempted to stunt its growth.
Think about the weeds
That covered its glow and
Made its presence nearly invisible.

Whenever you see a
Bright and colorful flower,
Think about how it nearly withered away,
Had it not been for that one raindrop.

Think about how it
Withstood pressure,
As harmful substances
Were thrown its way.

Think about that
Unfertile soil that
Almost strangled
It to death.

Think about the
Growing pains of bursting out,
Springing forth and
Breaking free from a place

It once considered home.

Think about its journey of evolution;
Becoming and blossoming
Into what others doubted
It would become.

A flower too, has a story,
And soon you'll discover
That it's a reflection of yours.

My Journey

One day I'll tell you about my journey,
While sipping palm wine
And eating sugar palm nuts.

About the war years
That stole my childhood;
About going to school
Under the sound of gunshots.

About fleeing to a foreign land
Whose language I couldn't speak,
And having to learn it in the end.

About conquering fear
Every time it shows its face,
Breaking free from societal limitations,
And living in God's purpose for me.

One day I'll tell you about my journey;

About the high mountains and low valleys,
And how long it took
To figure out this thing called life;
And finally realizing that
One never really figures it out.

Until then,
Let me tell you about the beauty of this land
I call home, LIB,
The place to be.

Step Out Girl

Wipe your tears,
Dry your eyes,
Pat your back,
And put on that smile.

Brace yourself,
It's not the end of the world;
Still ahead, are people to meet,
And places to go,
You're not even half way there yet.

Is that familiar voice
In your head telling you to quit?
No!
That's not a choice;
You must not settle for less.

Save your tears for joyful times,
When you'd need them most.
Are there chains that hold you down?
Break them,
And step out girl!

Are your traffic lights red all the time?
In the depth of your soul,
Are many green lights;
Find them, turn them on,
And step out girl!

A Thousand Lives

I've been a wife
Without being married.

A mother,
Without bearing a child.

Someone's enemy,
Without committing an offense.

A citizen of a faraway country,
Only through the flight of my dreams.

Someone's best friend,
From the consoling words I write.

Someone's wife-to-be,
All in their dreams.

I've been a president, a pilot,
A preacher, a market woman,
A pen-pen driver.

All through shared experiences,
And the common thread of humanity;

I've lived a thousand lives,
Yet only one.

Woman On A Mission

A mission to win.
A mission to rule.
A mission to rise.
A mission to thrive.

When surrounded by charcoal beams,
She sees bright city lights.
When dust and darkness fill the air,
She sees star lit cities and crisp clean skies.
To many, the vision seems unclear,
But she pushes and stays the course till the end.

This woman is on a mission.

A mission to conquer.
A mission to shine.
A mission to lift up.
A mission to build up.

Through waterside market,
She foresees glamorous shops,
Flagship stores, and a shopping district,
Where shopping is something to relish,
Instead of an everyday hustle.

This woman is on a mission.

A mission to shatter walls
Of poverty and stagnation.
A mission to bring a smile
To a hurting heart.
A mission to embrace children
In search of hope.
A mission to change the world,
One girl at a time.

A mission to bring pride
To a nation struggling to heal.

And when the mission is accomplished,
She'll embark upon the journey all over again.
This woman is on a once in a life time mission,
Whose story will be told long after she's gone.

My Body, My Pride

I hear you scheming, planning,
And plotting to invade this space—my space.
With your deceptive charm,
You send forth a fortified army to
Snatch away my treasured possession;
My body.

When it's dark outside,
You make secret plans
And set up an army;
Your soldiers—lies, alcohol, sex and money.
You empower to launch an attack
On my precious gem.

To you I look defenseless,
My curves make me look weak and helpless;
But I will not surrender,
And that will be your reminder.

When you get closer,
You'll soon discover
I have my own army;
My mind to think,
And calculate your moves.

My hands to work
And give me what you think I cannot afford;
My words, to dismantle your ego—your fortress,
My light will blind and disarm you.

I'm equipped to withstand your pressure,
Because I carry a treasure.
Didn't you know that
I'm a temple and you must bow in worship?

48

You'll tremble
At the sound of my voice;
Raising your hands in surrender.
This is my divine treasure;
My body, my pride.

Suddenly

It all happened so suddenly.

Didn't know that my heart
Would melt from the look in his eyes.
Didn't know that my head
Would swing at the sound of his voice.
Didn't know that
I could get betrayed by my emotions.

Oh, the sensation.

He kissed my hand,
Like the queen I am;
All too gently and regally divine.
I felt a strange feeling,
Could it be love or lust?

I anticipated the former,
But it happened oh so suddenly.

Nothing Can Tell How I Feel

Words cannot express,
Breeze cannot blow,
Actions cannot tell,
How I feel about you.

Birds cannot sing,
Stories cannot tell,
Lips cannot speak,
What's planted deep down
In my heart for you.

Mountains, hills, valleys,
And streams.
Rivers, lakes, oceans,
The land and trees;
Will never tell what I feel for you.

My heart dances and soars
With melodies for you.
My hips swing from side to side
Because of you.

I wear an eternal smile for you.
I love you,
And nothing can ever tell
What's planted
Deep in my soul for you.

You're the man of my throne;
King of my world.

Painful Christmas

I sit here,
Heart filled with grief,
Eyes flooded with tears;
I should be singing,
But I'm here weeping.

"Season's greetings,"
I hear them say;
"Merry, Merry, Christmas,"
But all I hear is painful Christmas.

From a far, I hear children's laughter,
But to me, they sound like cries.
The meals look delicious,
But to me, they taste sour and awful.

No gifts from Santa,
No kiss to ease away the pain;
Only Oldman Beggar[7] and company,
Beating their drums and begging the day away.

"Compliments of the season,"
They keep telling me;
I wish they could just say
"Season's condolences,"
Painful, tearful, Christmas.

---

7   Oldman Beggar - in Liberia, Xmas entertainers who are
awarded money by spectators for their dancing

Beyond Doubts

You start,
They laugh.

You move forward,
They doubt.

You don't quit,
They ignore.

You persevere,
They watch.

You rise,
They're shocked.

You win,
They become believers.

They Called Me Mama Africa
(Memories from Miss World 2006)

They called me Mama Africa;
The fun one,
The loud one,
The colorful one,
With an extra touch of country spice,
The bubbly one,
The not-afraid-to-stand-out one.

They called me Mama Africa;
The feisty one,
The fire in her belly one,
The dancing-on-the-bus-
Till-that-chaperone-who-doesn't-smile-
Smiles one,
The graceful one.

They called me Mama Africa;
The Miriam Makeba head gear adorned one,
The leader,
The trendsetter,
The non-conformist,
The creative,
The compassionate,
The queen of Zota exported to the world.

They called me Mama Africa.

Her Mind Grew Wings

Sealed possibilities,
Caged dreams,
Dark walls of fear,
Doubts and uncertainties,
Buried voices and chained feet.

Bleak Surroundings,
Mirrored by poverty,
Starvation and greed.

Captured, when she'd attempt to soar,
Silenced, whenever she'd try to speak,
Finally a bright spark—unleashed!

And so, her mind grew wings;
Wings to fly beyond obstacles,
The norms, the past,
And the familiar.

To the stairway
Of who she'd become,
Wings above barriers,
Into a realm of possibilities
And fulfilled dreams.

Wings to set sail,
Chart a new path,
And sing a new song.

A renewed song,
Of wholeness,
Healing and triumph,
Echoing for generations to come.

Discuss Your Life

Discuss art.
Discuss music.
Discuss education.

Discuss poetry.
Discuss intelligence.
Discuss books.

Discuss nature.
Discuss business.
Discuss food.

Discuss movies.
Discuss travel.
Discuss style.

Discuss development.
Discuss love.
Discuss culture.

Discuss innovation.
Discuss progress.
Discuss creativity.

And above all,
Discuss YOUR LIFE,
And how you can become a better YOU.

Education, I Cherish You

Education,
You're like a golden sword
In a warrior's hand
That always keeps him victorious.

Education, I cherish you.
You're like a precious stone
One cannot afford to throw away,
But keeps gazing at,
Beholding its mysterious beauty.

Education, I cherish you.
You've made me to stand up
Like a heroine against the rough,
And disastrous hands of ignorance,
Poverty and disease, with wisdom.

Education, I cherish you.
The well of knowledge is deep;
It is the buckets
We bring to it that are small.

Through education,
I've seen what is true,
And practiced that which is good.
I've seen and numbered the stars
Through education.

Education, don't you ever leave my side,
I need you in this world
To walk through life's tremendous journey;
Education, I truly cherish you.

You Remain 16 To Me

As the days and months go by,
As the moments pass us by,
You remain 16 to me.

Your raucous laughter
And enchanting smile,
Your glowing and knowing eyes,
Spring forth passion.

Your soul is "16,"
And your mind "80,"
Calming, yet vigorous.

Your presence makes me
Want to jump around,
And play under the rain.

Your words of wisdom make me
Want to dwell in your heart.
When I look at you,
I don't see age—I see youth.

I see a man created to rule!
With you, all the simple things
In life are precious.

They say, "Age is nothing but a number."
You, my darling,
Make that so true.

You're my friend with whom
I want to do the wildest
And craziest things.

Your soul is "16",
Your mind is like precious sapphire.
With every passing day,
You remain "16" to me.

You're endowed from above,
Oh, you handsome "16"
You'll always be "16" to me!

My Child I Never Got to Meet

Sometimes I wander,
Far, far, away,
On a journey
To no particular place.

I land on the shores of your memory,
And drift to the sound of your heartbeat;
Rhythms that once charmed me,
Feelings that once awakened me,
Now haunt me.

Changes, once ever so present,
Soon vanished.
I sit still to the longing
Of the calm you once brought me.

I reminisce
About your tiny feet I didn't get to see,
Your full bright eyes I couldn't stare into,
Hearty cries I never got to hear;
I wonder what you would've looked like?

Would you have had
Your mother's piercing eyes and brilliance,
Or, your father's charm and wit?

Would you have been mouthy,
Like your grandmother's last born,
Or caring and motherly like her firstborn?

Would you have been a dreamer,
A doer, or a do-gooder?
Would you have been feisty,
A leader with wisdom-laden words?

Would you have been a wanderer
In search of yourself,
And a deeper meaning of life?

These words, sprinkled on your memory,
Now angels that guide and console me;
Until you pass my way again someday,
My child, I await.

Sorry I Left You Behind

Once we sat on the same bench,
Ate from the same bowl,
And drank from the same cup.
Inseparable we seemed,
Dreams intertwined and plans overlapped.
It seemed we were headed
In the same direction.

We'd drown in pettiness,
And dream to the limits of
What our eyes could see;
An eagle had ceased to soar,
A gem had lost its sparkle,
And so I journeyed through myself,
And back to where we sat.

And I realized we weren't
On the same frequency,
That we weren't headed
In the same direction,
So I decided to walk my own path,
And soar in pursuit of my destiny and purpose.

So, sorry I left you behind,
Sorry, I parted ways,
With the dreams we once shared in that barrel.
Cluttered with hopelessness,
Frustration and shattered hopes,
To a bigger vision and calling.

Sorry I broke free from the lies,
And narrowness of the world we knew;
In search of a bigger world out there,
One in which I truly belonged.
Sorry I became complicated,

Unable to be boxed in or labeled,
Sorry, you felt we were headed
In the same direction,
When all I saw was a transit point.

Sorry I lost you, but oh,
I'm not really sorry,
Because, in losing you,
I found me;
Sorry, I left you behind.

When Love Is Not Enough

You see blue sunny skies,
He sees dark and cloudy nights.
You see blissful forever;
A future, a family, a home,
But all he sees is you,
Void of commitment.

You see promise and hope,
He sees raunchy and passionate nights.
You love with all your might to secure his heart,
But every ounce you give,
Sends your heart falling into shreds.

You see a beautiful ending,
But all he sees is a hot and steamy today;
So what do you do, my darling,
When love is not enough?

Do you wrap the pieces
Of your broken heart, in a box,
Tie it up with a ribbon and
Throw it into the sea?

Do you cry oceans
That fill up barrels to show
How much you care?
Do you stay and
Lose a piece of you,
While masking your pain?

Or do you unwrap that box,
Empty the barrel and
Pour onto yourself the
Biggest love you've ever known?

Do you take the brokenness
And build a bridge to cross over
To a brighter side?

Do you stay and die slowly
On the inside while you're still alive?
What do you do
When love is not enough?

Waiting

Waiting,
Waiting,
Waiting!

Waiting for this,
Waiting for that.
Waiting for him,
Waiting for her.

How long will you keep waiting?
When all you're waiting for is you?

We Are Here
(*On women's persistence and resilience in the face of hurdles*)

Throw us under the bus,
We'll get up unscathed.

Give us empty words,
We'll turn them into weapons.

Silence us,
Our actions will speak louder.

Chain us,
We'll form a unifying force.

Glass ceilings remain,
But above, around and beyond them, we shall soar.

Woman Power, power like no other,
Feminine, yet divine.

You'll see us,
You'll hear us.

We will speak up,
We are here.

That Thing Called Fear

That thing called fear,
    It holds your mind in bondage;
        Your thoughts held captive.

It strangles your dreams
    Before they see daylight;
        Keeps you in chains.

Yet you're free,
    And attends your funeral;
        While you're still alive.

I Cannot Help But Shine

Are my rays so bright
    That they could leave you blind?

Do my glitters spill
    All over you when I walk by?

You need not be surprised,
    I outshine the sun, moon and stars.

Just take it all in stride,
    I cannot help but shine.

Make Your Behind-the-Scenes Beautiful

That place beneath the glitz and glamor;
Far away from the spotlight,
Littered with failures, tears,
Sleepless nights, confusion and heartbreaks.

That place no amount of makeup,
Smiles or filter can conceal;
That place where you sit alone,
Scattered, shattered and broken.

That place where reality greets you,
And looks at you boldly in the eye;
That place only you can confront,
That place no one sees, but you.

Make it beautiful.

To Love An ECOWAS Passport Holder

It takes someone with a heart of steel,
Lined with the purest patience to love,
Truly love, an ECOWAS[8] passport holder.

Lonely days and boring nights,
Separated by flights,
And a thousand miles.

Only hope is, that visa appointment
That turns into a vacation
Before THE vacation;
One can't just take off and fly,
16-hour layovers.

Stuck in an airport somewhere,
And never getting to see
The surrounding city.

To love an ECOWAS passport holder,
Planning trips one year in advance
Becomes a way of life,
And flying, a miracle.

The world seems oceans away,
And dreams seem caged.
It takes someone who's willing
To fly to the end of the earth,
To find their West African gem,
A treasure like none other.

Prepare for an adventure,
Unique in itself,
When you love, truly love,
An ECOWAS passport holder.

---

8   ECOWAS: Economic Community of West African
States

Prayer Of Humility

When I fly high and touch the clouds,
And think I can make it,
Through my own power and might;
Lord, take me back to that place.

When pride tries to sneak
Its way into my heart,
Making me think the glory is mine,
When it's solely yours;
Take me back to that simple place.

When I boast of my doings and strength,
Instead of acknowledging your omnipotence;
Lord, take me back to that tranquil place.

When the riches of this world cloud my focus,
Taking my eyes off your heavenly prize
Of peace and abundance;
Lord, take me back to that place.

When I look at other human beings,
And ignore your image of love within them;
Lord, take me back to that place.

Clip my wings, so I can fly only for you.
Tame my tongue, to speak only of your
Wonders and love.
Blind my eyes from evil, so I can only see
The good you've placed in everyone.

Close my ears,
So I can listen keenly to your word.
Take me back to that humble place,
Where I realized I was nothing without you.

Even If

Even If I cry, I won't die.
Even if I bend, I won't break.
Even if I'm lonely, I won't crawl.
I know my worth.

Even if you leave, I won't chase.
I'll gladly embrace my solitude,
And build a ladder to my dreams.

Even if it rains, I'll dream of sunny skies.
Even if my heart breaks,
I'll learn to heal and trust again.

You may see me fail, but I won't lose.
I'll stop, but I'll shape up,
And move on again;
This time a lot stronger.

Even if I'm misunderstood,
I won't change;
This world you see,
Is more complex than you think.

Even if there are dark days,
I'll be that ray of light
In someone's sky.

My Own Identity

I

My mother did not get on a boat
With a name as sleek as okra on your tongue;
She did not know privilege
That opened every door,
She did not live in a mansion
Overlooking the ocean,
But built us a cushion
Through her hard work with pride.
She did not inherit wealth,
And easy access to the world,
And did not dine with kings and queens.

II

She is the queen, regal and adorned with grace;
She carved out her own space
Through diligence and sacrifice,
And in watching her toil,
I courageously picked up the torch
And embarked upon my own journey.

III

I forged my identity;
Not one based upon my father's rank in the society,
Or by how many accounts,
Or properties he owned.
Not one built from arrogance and vanity,
Or one of entitlement.
But an identity of integrity,
Diligence and perseverance.
A story inclusively written;
A story from Zota, Yeakporwa and Kweletai,
Of joys and triumphs,

Of high and lows.

IV

An identity of strength,
Bearing the untold stories;
Of those who built something
Out of nothing,
And made being broken whole.

The Glorious Stage

Step onto the glorious stage.
Step with vigor.
Step with valor.
Step courageously.
Step triumphantly.
Step oh, step!

Step on the stage
And take your place.
Step on the stage
And own your shine;
For time will one day pass you by.

Step as your mind soars.
Step as your dreams fly.
Step to your heart's rhythm.
Step to your soul's longings.
Step with a song on your lips.
Step while swaying your hips.

Savor the sunsets.
Cherish your freedom.
Relish the journey,
For life is a glorious stage;
And we're here to play our part,
And bow till eternity.

Wish Of A Dreamer

I wish I could tell you to dream;
Dream with your eyes open,
Dream with your eyes closed,
Dream staring at blue skies,
Dream watching sunsets.

I wish I could tell you,
Dreams have no boundaries;
No borders and barriers,
And that your only limitation is you.

I wish I could tell you
To define your path,
And be convicted in your definition;
Whatever that definition is.

Oh I wish I could tell you,
That to follow societal labels
Is the undoing of your purpose.

I wish I could tell you
How isolated,
And rocky the road to success is.

I wish I could tell you that,
All dreams without hard work
Are just that—dreams;
Like dust blown in the wind.

Oh dare to dream,
But above all,
Plan, act, and
Get off the wish wagon.

On A Rainy Day

On a rainy day,
I think of you;
I think of you being next to me,
I think of your warmth.

On a rainy day,
Your smile shines through me
Like a beaming sunlight.

I think of the passion
We always share,
I think of the closeness
That binds us together in love.

On a rainy day,
All I think about is you.
And as the cool wind blows,
I feel your hands
Sprinkling magic all over me.

Then I roll around my bed,
Curl up and go to sleep.

Friends Of The World
(Inspired by Miss World)

They laughed,
Echoing cheer and peace,
Sailing my soul to a tranquil place.

Beaming smiles,
Glowing and adorned
With the creator's craft,
Left and right—beauties.

Global beauties;
Beauties nature has yet to behold;
Majestic steps thriving
Towards a glorious throne.

Closeness and warmth
That created special bonds;
Bonds which brought forth friendships
To last a lifetime.

Beautiful and sacred memories,
The studded crown and graceful waves,
Regal steps; memories too precious to forget.

Goodbye, as always,
Was sad to say;
As the good times hurriedly faded away,
We had to go our separate ways.

But they remained friends of the world,
And cherished friends of my heart.

Tell Your Story

The old ones.
The new ones.
The recycled ones.
The forgotten ones.
The ignored ones.

Stories from yesterday
Hidden between the pages,
Of life's hustle and toil;
Stories from yesteryears,
Buried under rocks and concrete floors.

Tell your story.
The sad ones.
The treasured ones.
The painful ones.
The liberating ones.

Stories of voices too caged to speak,
Stories of generations
On whose shoulders you stand.

Tell your story.
The heart-wrenching ones.
The lung-dancing ones.
The mind-boggling ones.
The hip-swinging ones.

Stories of triumph washed on distant shores,
Stories of warriors,
Who conquered kingdoms and thrones.

Tell your story.
Part your lips and let them speak.
Wink your eyes and let them blink.

Unearthed your voice and let it ring.

Tell your story,
In high melodies and low symphonies,
Through walks and dance,
Through anguish and grief,
Through laugher and cries,
On mountains high and valleys low.

Tell it loudly.
Tell it slowly.
Tell it softly.
Tell it with voice shaking,
Trembling, shouting.

But tell it.

Stories of Djor River.
Stories of Kpatawee.
You own it.
You worked for it.
You sacrificed for it.

So tell it.

Tell it proudly.
Tell it majestically.
Tell it while standing tall.
Tell it bowing low.

But tell it.

Tell it. Tell it. Tell it.
Because, my darling,
Who will tell it, if you don't?

These Daughters Of Ours

These daughters of ours
Will break down walls,
Open new doors,
And walk down the aisles of their dreams.
They shall sing new songs,
Visit distant shores,
And erase the shame of history's wrath.
They shall cry a different cry,
And live a life whose vision we bore.

These daughters of ours
Will take our names to faraway lands
We may never see,
And place them on the lips
Of kings and queens.
They shall rewrite old stories,
Unearthed glorious legacies,
And carry the spears of warriors
Long buried upon their shoulders.

These daughters of ours
Will change one sided narratives,
Dream their own dreams,
And make their own rules.
They shall find the answers,
Unfold mysteries and soar limitlessly.
These daughters of ours
Are the answers the world
Has been longing for.

My Sisters In Goals, Strength And Prayers

Dear sisters,
Seasons have come and gone,
And so have love and loved ones;
We've lost and gained,
We've laughed and cried,
But you, my sisters,
Are rare gems to me.

You've stood firm through raging storms,
Changes, stages, and levels;
Celebrated the wins, not only the gains,
And relished in the joys of dreams fulfilled.

You've taught me
What blessing there is in letting go,
And how glorious it is to start anew;
We've shared the lessons and blessings,
And reminded each other to shine
When life forced us to shrink.

You've honored my gifts,
Cherished my wit and,
Encouraged me to soar;
You've prayed me up,
Held my hand and remembered me,
Not only for what I can offer,
But what I mean to you.

My sisters in goals, strength and prayers;
Here's to working, rising,
And wining together.

The Lonestar Rant

Excuse me ladies and gentlemen,
This is not a diss, this is a rant;
It's a 2016 Lonestar rant,
Fasten your seatbelts!

When it rains mediocrity and corruption,
Ignorance and fear become the umbrella,
Shielding us, un-shielding us,
Exposing us to greed.

Broken dreams littered across graveyards,
Drinking spots and Ataye shops
Create delusional PHDs,
The Palava Huts make you sound smarter,
Louder than Pay-Me Weah's mic.

Ah! The meal of the day is,
A street side banquet of spaghetti,
Beans and cucumber—ah mayonnaise;
What strange things!

The fragrance of that yellow something
Bursting from broken pipes;
As we hold our noses tight,
Oh, I thought fragrances were meant to appease,
But all this does is displease.

Passenger 57 reminds you of a movie night?
Oh! That's a leg-dragging,
And bag-snatching night;
Don't mind that oldma
Seated proudly at the back.

Whatever happened to kukalay kukatunon[9]?

---

9   "We all are one" Kpelle language spoken in Liberia.

Oh well, the freestyle policies
Are draining our resources like fantasy;
The only way your dreams come true,
Is when you're ridden majestically
To Center Street covered with wood and flowers.

And your eye cries failure,
Your nose runs fear,
Your ears hear defeat.
When friends try to stagnate you,
All because their definition of success
Does not resonate with you.

When the gold chain
Takes you on the money chase,
"Deeds not words",
But their deeds have
Drowned our words and actions;
Forcing young girls to
Make old schools their financial plans.

Oh wait!
What happened to the gold chain
And cell phone era?
Well, I tip my hat off,
Cause at least some of my sisters are
On the Carey just to make it to the classrooms.

When the emperor knows he's naked,
But refuses to get dressed,
What do you do?
Rewind time and bring back normal days?
Oh no! The last time I checked,
It was the same spilled milk
On Charlie King's stairs.

The future looks bleak;
It's 2016 and we're still taking bucket baths

With the loads still smiling at us;
LEC is disco dancing,
And water sewer is acting like dew,
While missiles fly on your roof, oh excuse!

When I Turned 30

They said the sky would fall and turn gray,
The oceans would dry up,
And life's adventures would end
When I turned 30.

They said the invisible clock would stop ticking,
And that I, still so young and in my prime,
Would seize to bloom,
Lose my youthful zest,
And be called "old"

That life would have passed me by,
And that I, so accustomed to blossoming,
Would wither and fade away;
That without kids and a husband,
I'd have no identity or place,
All when I turned 30.

I heard that the goddess of beauty
Would dim my light and lock up its glow,
And my eternal misery would unfold;
That my dreams would seize to soar,
And my mind would lose its brilliant spark.

Now here I am, standing tall,
Shedding those myths and lies;
Unweaving those words
And weaving my own path and truth.

My truth; discarding labels and disrupting timelines,
Working on my clock of compassion;
On God's time, not man's.
Yes, 30 came, looked me in the eye
And said, "Girl, let's conquer the world!"

On Planes

Crowded airports and occupied seats,
Unsaid prayers and unsung songs.
Full flights are empty;
Pillowy clouds, greatness unmatched.

Tasty meals, served by strangers,
Radiant smiles, casual connections,
Vulnerability—a bigger power in control.
Strangers from across the world,
Yet citizens of the mid-air skies.

Floating, dreaming, and yearning.
Home is here, but way over there.
Praying, waiting, hoping—
Calming the nerves.

That feeling you get,
When your emotions are lost between the clouds;
A symphony of prayer wrapped in thoughts,
Only when you're on planes.

Riding Through Africa

Riding through Africa,
A journey across mountains,
Valleys, rivers, and plains has begun;
Buckle up and journey with me.

I make a stop to the clear waters
Of Liberia's Lake Piso on my Pen-Pen,
And hear them say Ya-kunay!

Then hit the streets of Naija
On my shining Okada,
"Aye Igwe, make we run things!"

I ride peacefully to the Gold Coast of Ghana
To see my Odo,
And to eat some banku and tilapia,
On my Aboboyaa.

I head to the east side,
Making a stop in Kenya,
Uganda and Tanzania
On my Bodaboda.

I cross over to Rwanda and Somalia on my Moto,
Make a jolly stop in Malawi on my Tuk Tuk,
And head down south
To eat some Pap in Zimbabwe,
On my Mdududu.

I'm chilling as a Zulu South African princess
On my Sthuthuthu.
Pen-pen, Okada, Aboboyaa,
Bodaboda, Moto, Tuk Tuk,
Mdududu, Sthuthuthu,
Come on let's ride through Africa!

Voice In A Hole

Six feet under,
Their voices were buried
In the cold dark earth,
They sang no more;
Silenced by darkness and filth,
Maggots, bugs and worms,
Their only companions.

Amid rainfall and sunshine,
They lay still—no word uttered.
Their lips were plastered—they couldn't speak.
They longed for the day
When their songs would be heard.

Their hands were cuffed—they couldn't wave,
No trace of light,
It seemed hope was completely lost.
Though hungry, optimism filled their bellies,
Knowing liberation was assured.

When Ellen Johnson-Sirleaf defied
The norms of male dominance in leadership,
And became Africa's first female president,
Their voices resurrected.

When Waris Dirie escaped
The bondage of Female Genital Mutilation
And child marriage at the tender age of 13,
Becoming one of Africa's
First international supermodels,
Their voices resurrected!

When Oprah Winfrey overcame
Child abuse and adversity,
Becoming the world's first

Black woman billionaire,
Their voices resurrected!

When 3 female Nobel laureates,
Johnson-Sirleaf, Gbowee, and Karman,
Went against all odds,
Breaking the chains and amplifying the voices
Of women across the world,
Their voices resurrected!

Awakened voices;
Vibrant and hopeful,
Buried no more.

Love Like This

This love, a love like this;
A love with care,
A love with cheer,
The warm feeling
That brings healing.

I've never been in haste
To taste a love like this.

Never imagined
A love without reservation,
Cherished like a treasure,
And pampered beyond imagination.

Heavenly bliss!
Awakened by a kiss.
Heart-warming and soothing,
Genuine and divine.

I never, ever imagined
A love like this.

The Day I Found You

The day I found you,
Life's true meaning was revealed.
The day I found you,
No one will ever understand
How my heart smiled with warmth
From the look in your eyes.

The day I found you,
Your smile engulfed
My entire soul with passion,
I envisaged spending forever,
And days after with you.

The day I found you,
Just one word uttered,
Took me a thousand miles into paradise.

Oh that day,
The day I found you,
All my dreams came true.

Liberia

Liberia,
The rising continent's Lonestar,
The west coast's hidden gem,
And Liberians' pride.

Rise again,
Shine again.
Bring back the glory of yesteryears
Shielded by war, disease,
Poverty and greed.

Bring back the strength
Burrowed from you,
By those who once sought you
In search of a home.

Africa's "Little America",
How long will you keep hiding
Behind an identity that is not your own?

How long will you keep roaming,
And running in search
Of all that you already possess?

Liberia,
Home of every black man,
Every African,
And every person in search of freedom—
Home to nations.

Shine like the star that you are;
Awaken and rise above the shadows
That have held you captive.

Liberia,
You're all Liberians have,
Their pride and joy;
Rise and lead them into a pasture of peace.
You've risen before;
Shatter the walls of complacency,
And rise beyond the laurels of your past.

"Deeds not words"

You've spoken for too long,
Now it's time to get to work.
Your people are proud of you,
They believe in you.

Reconcile them,
Bring peace and unity amongst them.
Develop the land beyond the forests;
Rise up and take your place.
Scars are medals of triumph,
Wear them with pride and conquer.

Life

Life;
The blossoming of a flower,
The cry of a newborn baby,
A vapor of smoke,
The chirping of birds,
A stranger's soulful cries.

Life;
Chattering children,
A wedding feast, and a funeral miles away,
A heart bursting with love,
A broken-hearted pillow soaked in tears.

Laughter here—cries there,
A new birth—a last breath,
Stages, events and happenings;
Each, at its own time and pace,
Relish it, lest life passes you by.

A True Friend

A true friend
Has a cushion in their heart for you;
Laughs and cries with you,
And never competes.

A true friend
Is happy when you succeed;
Listens and uplifts,
And corrects you
When you're wrong.

A true friend
Stays when others go;
Doesn't undermine you,
And is a safe place
Away from home.

A true friend
Empowers and cultivates;
Celebrates and elevates,
And brings calm in your storm.

A true friend
Is compassionate;
Considerate, and
A divine blessing from above.

Under Ducor Skies

Their cries were loud,
So everyone could hear,
They lay flat under the rain and blazing sun,
Singing one song, crying one cry—PEACE!

Through hungry days and tumultuous nights,
They bowed under Ducor skies;
Waiting for the clouds
To pour down rain of peace.

They could hear their children's cries,
Pain filled their eyes;
But still they kept hope alive,
And remained under Ducor skies.

The dusty ground became a sacred shrine,
So many prayers offered;
For a lost land and people
Seeking direction and hope.

Under Ducor skies,
They stood in peaceful defiance;
Until their hopes
Of the birth of a new nation
Were finally realized.

Married To Me

From strength to strength,
Parting ways with weakness,
Sorrows and tears,
Till success takes me higher,
Oh yes, I must!
I'm married to me.

Walking down the aisle
Of my greater tomorrow,
Smiling radiantly and
Leaving behind the sorrows of yesterday;
I'm married to me.

Vowing to rid this life of tear-filled pillows,
Negativity and abuse,
Vowing to be my own strength
In sunny and gloomy weather,
I'm married to me.

Parting ways with sickness and poverty,
Saying, "Yes, I do", to success and possibilities,
And a future waiting to bloom,
I'm married to me.

From greatness to greatness,
To live abundantly, wholly,
Confidently and fearlessly;
All the days of my life.

Yes, I will,
I'm married to me.

I'm Liberian

A sigh,
A gasp,
A side eye,
A breath of fresh air.

Liberian.

Inhale it,
Exhale it,
Then say it slowly, Li-be-rian.

A bowl of Palm Butter and rice
To get you on your toes,
An extravagant attire,
Turning heads and inviting stares.

Liberian.

Fire in my veins, hospitality in my embrace,
Unpredictably predictable,
Scars, wounds and beauty;
All wrapped up in one.

Liberian.

The genesis of your freedom
Enlightened, misunderstood,
And beautifully flawed;
Roll your eyes when you say it,
Suck your teeth to nail it,
Open your heart to feel it.

The best jollof rice,
Africa's most beautiful woman,
rising above her complexities.

Say it,
Get used to it,
You've gotta shine your eyes to truly see it.

I'm Liberian.

Let's Rebuild Liberia Together
(*Miss Liberia winning poem*)

For centuries, Africa was covered with darkness;
Darkness from the oppression of slavery,
Humiliation, and ignorance.
Beyond the dark clouds came
This shining Lonestar that brightened her path,
And became a beacon of hope
For the whole of Africa—Liberia!

She declared her independence in 1847,
And earned the respect of African nations
And the world at large.

She has left positive footprints in history,
Acquired great achievements,
And has faced numerous challenges,
Including the devastation of war,
And is now left with the
Heavy task of reconstruction.

Liberia's reconstruction
Cannot be left only with the government
And the international community;
We all can play a part
In rebuilding Liberia.

And this is how we can begin:
Police, Liberia needs you,
You can use the training
Acquired from the United Nations Mission in Liberia
To contribute to enhancing the security system
Of our country and make it crime free.

Students, "Precious Jewels" of our nation,
Use the knowledge you acquire in schools

To broaden your horizon and
Play your part in rebuilding Liberia.

The Armed Forces of Liberia (AFL),
Liberia needs you to serve
In the vanguard of defense
To protect and defend the sovereignty of the state.

Ex-combatants,
There's no need to feel isolated anymore,
Liberia needs you.
Use the skills you have acquired
To restructure your lives,
And join everyone else to rebuild Liberia.

Farmers, you're the backbone of the nation;
Be empowered to go back to the soil
And grow more food,
Enhance the productivity of Liberia,
Making it self-sufficient.

Lawyers, guardians of our nation,
Ensure that the rule of law
Takes its course without fear or favor;
Do away with the culture of impunity.

Religious leaders, conscience of our nation,
Serve as a symbol of unity;
Thus bringing our nation together.

Politicians, brains of our nation;
Lead with distinction and patriotism
To ensure the development,
Unity and progress of our nation.

With smiles on our faces,
And with un-diminishing faith and courage,
We can all unite as Liberians

In spite of our tribes,
Religious or political affiliations;
And adapt the developmental slogan
Of our late president, Rev. Dr. William R. Tolbert,

"Total involvement for higher heights!"
And work towards building
A stairway of higher heights for Liberia.

The African Dream

Why wither away in the land overseas?
I'm here at home feeling the dust and breeze.
I go through my hustle with relative ease,
No stress over bills or mortgage
To keep Uncle Sam pleased.

I awake to the ocean breeze,
Go about my day to the beat of drums and sasa,
Dawn ushers in a golden sunrise,
A promise of a new day awaits.

The land mesmerizes me.
The culture captivates me.
That's always the feeling,
When you're living the African dream.

Liberating, exhilarating, soothing.
The African dream is freedom.
The African dream is resilience.
The African dream is hope.
The African dream is here.
The African dream is now.

Take Me To Kpatawee

Oh weee! Oh way yooo!
Take me to Kpatawee;
Ma Yamah's red oil soup
Is always in my dreams,
Gbarnga highway
Is screaming my name.

Uncle Saah's taxi's waiting,
As we happily hop in,
Redlight market's noisy,
But it is so, just as we know it.

Highway breeze;
Palm trees wave their branches,
Palm wine sellers standing by,
Refill your gallon they will.

I yearn to see the rushing waters glide
Through rocks as we chat
And laugh our time by.

Oh weee!
Take me to Kpatawee!
Phebe hospital is nearby;
Cuttington's book people wave happily at me.

I don't care how long it takes,
Just take me to Kpatawee.

Not An Ordinary Woman

I'm not an ordinary woman,
I'm a different kind of woman.
A woman with a purpose.
A woman with vision.
I dream, I pray, I work.

Setbacks don't intimidate me,
Failures don't humiliate me;
I break boundaries,
Weave pain into purpose,
And dance to the beat of my own drum.

I'm bold, confident and secured,
Not out of arrogance;
But in the security of WHOSE I am,
I'm not an ordinary woman.

I'm a leader,
Following God's blueprint for me.
I'm a planet shaker,
A game changer,
A legacy builder.

A woman whose light
Paves the way for generations,
An exceedingly blessed woman;
I'm not an ordinary woman.

"Birthing books, touching lives,
and walking down the aisle of my dreams."

~ Patrice Juah

Patrice D. Juah

About the Author

Ms. Patrice Juah is a dynamic and multifaceted media and communications professional with proven consulting skills and expertise in strategic communications, public relations, conducting specialized trainings, public speaking and digital content development. As the founder and Managing Partner of MOIE, a diversified media social enterprise, Patrice remains committed to improving the communications sector and entrepreneurial opportunities across Africa. She is an accomplished author and poet, with literary works covering a wide range of themes to include personal life experiences, women's empowerment, and humor.

Ms. Juah is a 2014 Mandela Washington Fellow, former Miss Liberia and Girl's Education Advocate, that has consistently strived to motivate and empower young Liberian women by supporting local non-profit organizations in their efforts to educate women on topics such as HIV/AIDs, teenage pregnancy, education, and workforce development. She's also a Columnist for Vital Woman Magazine UK's Girls' Empowerment Column and blogs for Tropics Magazine's Tropics Voices platform. Her most notable articles have been featured on PBS NewsHour, African Feminist Forum, Liberian Observer, AllAfrica, Conversations on Liberia and the Sea Breeze Journal of Contemporary Liberian Writings.

Ms Juah is the founder of the Martha Juah Educational Foundation and its Sexy Like A Book initiative, designed to inspire young women and girls to improve their perspective on reading, literacy & education.

Founded in 2015, *Sexy Like A Book* is Martha Juah Educational Foundation's academic initiative designed to inspire young women and girls to improve their perspective on reading, literacy & education.

PLEASE SUPPORT OUR CAUSE
MAKE A DONATION

Globally, many barriers continue to prevent girls from accessing quality education, as well as enrolling in, and completing secondary school. We believe that an improvement in the chances of the African girl having access to quality education, can only be achieved if we eliminate and break barriers such as female genital mutilation, child marriage, teenage pregnancy, poverty, violence against girls and women, the high cost of school etc., which continue to pose threats to, and prevent girls from accessing and completing primary and secondary school.

A 2016 UNESCO Institute for Statistics report states that girls are more likely than boys to never set foot in a classroom, despite all the efforts and progress made over the past two decades. According to UIS data, 15 million girls of primary-school age will never get the chance to learn to read or write in primary school compared to about 10 million boys. Over half of these girls—9 million—live in sub-Saharan Africa. In keeping with Goal 4 of the Sustainable Development Goals, which emphasizes the need to ensure inclusive and equitable quality education, and promote lifelong learning opportunities for all, Sexy Like A Book remains committed to combating the high rate of illiteracy in Liberia (52.4 %), through a holistic approach that engages girls, beyond the classrooms, harnessing their inborn talents, through mentorship, writing, public speaking, etiquette courses and community service etc. The overall goal is to equip them to meaningfully contribute to their communities and be active participants in decision-making on issues concerning their wellbeing.

We want to expand our reach to the 15 counties of Liberia, targeting girls (12-21 years old), particularly in the rural communities, through community outreach initiatives and awareness campaigns. If you're touched and would like to support our work, we encourage you to order our book Enchanting Voices and donate, to help us nurture and develop Liberia's next generation of leaders.

All proceeds from the book will go towards scaling up and strengthening our current projects.

"Alone we can do so little;
together we can do so much."

~ Helen Keller"

Order your copy today, to help us provide scholar-
ships and educational resources to Liberian girls,
particularly those in rural communities.

Available wherever books are sold.
Paperback and eBook.
Visit our website, www.sexlikeabook.com; to learn
more about this initiative. We need your support.

Martha Juah
Educational Foundation

Founded in 2008, Martha Juah Educational
Foundation is a registered not-for-profit organiza-
tion working to provide scholarships, mentorship
and innovative educational opportunities to girls in
rural Liberia.

www.ingramcontent.com/pod-product-compliance
Lightning Source LLC
Chambersburg PA
CBHW020918090426
42736CB00008B/685